ELLIOTT CARTER

OF CHALLENGE AND OF LOVE

Five Poems of John Hollander

for Soprano and Piano

HENDON MUSIC

BOOSEY & HAWKES

DISTRIBUTED BY

HAL•LEONARD®
CORPORATION

7777 W. BLUEMOUND RD. P.O. BOX 13819 MILWAUKEE, WI 53213

www.boosey.com
www.halleonard.com

Published by Hendon Music, Inc.,
a Boosey & Hawkes Company
35 East 21st Street
New York NY 10010

www.boosey.com

ISMN 979-0-051-93411-9

First printed 2009

Printed in U.S.A. and distributed by Hal Leonard Corporation, Milwaukee WI

Music engraving by William Holab

Commissioned by the Aldeburgh Foundation for Lucy Shelton
with funding provided by the Rex Foundation

First performed 23 June 1995 at the Aldeburgh Festival
by Lucy Shelton, soprano, and John Constable, piano

CONTENTS

	Page
1. HIGH ON OUR TOWER	1
2. UNDER THE DOME	10
3. *AM KLAVIER (at the Piano)*	19
4. QUATRAINS FROM HARP LAKE	26
5. END OF A CHAPTER	45

Please note that movements 2 and 3 may be interchanged.

Duration: 25 minutes

COMPOSER'S NOTE

John Hollander's poetry has fascinated me for many years because of its poetic skills, its awareness of our cultural past, and its wide-ranging modern expressivity. So when Lucy Shelton (whose performances of my work are superb) and the Aldeburgh Festival proposed that I write a cycle of songs for her, I accepted with great pleasure. The choice of the texts from many of Hollander's books and a typewritten script of "Quatrains from Harp Lake" (which John tells me is the Sea of Galilee) is basically focused around the character of that poem, with its brief, vividly contrasting quatrains that have an undercurrent of irony and deep anxiety, which is also found in the other four poems in different ways. The score was composed in the last months of 1994 in New York City.

—Elliott Carter

ANMERKUNG DES KOMPONISTEN

John Hollanders Poesie fasziniert mich schon lange wegen ihrer dichterischen Kunstfertigkeit, ihrer modernen Ausdrucksvielfalt und wegen des aus ihnen sprechenden Bewusstseins für unsere kulturelle Vergangenheit. Als Lucy Shelton (die meine Werke so hinreißend interpretiert) und das Aldeburgh Festival mich baten, einen Liederzyklus für sie zu schreiben, habe ich deshalb mit Freuden akzeptiert. Die Auswahl der Texte aus zahlreichen Büchern Hollanders sowie dem Maschinenskript „Quatrains from Harp Lake" (von dem John mir sagte, dass es sich um den Galiläischen See oder See Genezareth handelt) verdankt sich hauptsächlich dem Charakter dieses Gedichts mit seinen kurzen, lebhaft kontrastierenden Vierzeilern voll unterschwelliger Ironie und tiefer Beklemmung, die ähnlich auch in den vier anderen Gedichten mitschwingen. Die Partitur entstand in den letzten Monaten des Jahres 1994 in New York City.

—Elliott Carter

NOTE DU COMPOSITEUR

La poésie de John Hollander m'a fasciné durant des années en raison de son habileté poétique, de la conscience de notre passé culturel dont elle témoigne, et de sa vaste expressivité moderne. Alors, quand Lucy Shelton (dont l'interprétation de mes œuvres est superbe) et le Festival d'Aldeburgh m'ont proposé d'écrire un cycle de mélodies pour elle, j'ai accepté avec un immense plaisir. Le choix des textes, issus de différents livres de Hollander ainsi que d'une page dactylographié des « Quatrains de Harp Lake » (que John me dit être le Lac de Galilée), a été essentiellement déterminé par le caractère de ce poème-ci, dont les quatrains brefs, contrastant vivement entre eux, révèlent une ironie sous-jacente et une profonde anxiété, que l'on retrouve aussi, d'une façon différente, dans les quatre autres poèmes. La partition a été composée dans les derniers mois de 1994, à New York.

—Elliott Carter

VOCAL TEXTS

HIGH ON OUR TOWER

High on our tower
Where the winds were
Did my head turning
Turn yours,
Or were we burning
In the one wind?

Our wide stares pinned
To a spinning world,
We burned; my head,
Turning to yours
On that white tower,
Whirled high in fire.

All heights are our
Towers of desire;
All shaded spaces
Our valleys, enclosing
Now darkening places
Of unequal repose.

How tower-high were
Our whitest places
Where my head widely
Turned into yours
In the spaces of spinning,
In burning wind!

*How dark and far
Apart valleys are . . .*

UNDER THE DOME

That great, domed chamber, celebrated for its full choir
Of echoes: high among its shadowed vaults they cower
Until called out. What do echoes do when they reply?
Lie, lie, lie about what we cried out, about their own
Helplessness in the face of silence. What do they do
To the clear call that they make reverberate? *Berate,
Berate* it for its faults, its frangible syllables.
But in this dear cave we have discovered on our walks
Even a broken call resounds in all, and wild tales
We tell into the darkness return trimmed into truth.
Our talk goes untaunted: these are the haunts of our hearts,
Where I cry out your name. Hearing and overhearing
My own voice, startled, appalled, instructed, I rejoice.

AM KLAVIER (at the Piano)

The evening light dies down: all the old songs begin
To crowd the soft air, choiring confusedly.
Then above that sea of immense complexities
The clear tenor of memory I did not know
I had enters; like a rod of text held out by
A god of meaning, it governs the high, wayward
Waves of what is always going on in the world.
All that becomes accompaniment. And it is
What we start out with now: this is no time
To pluck or harp on antiquities of feeling.
These soft hammers give gentle blows to all their strings,
Blows that strike with a touch of challenge and of love.
Thus what we are, being sung against what we come
To be a part of, rises like a kind of light.

QUATRAINS FROM HARP LAKE

The thrumming waves of the lost lake had gone
    Into some kind of hiding since the spring.
His long yawn ceased to deafen, then switched on
    The sixty-cycle hum of everything.

Once we plucked ripened fruit and blossoms all
    Together from one branch, humming one note.
Spring from the water, shining fish, then fall
    In one unbroken motion into my boat!

The river whistled and the forest sang,
    Surprised, then pleased, that something had gone wrong.
The touches of your hands, your silence, rang
    Changes on the dull, joyous bells of song.

They stood tall, loving in the shade; the sunny
    Air withdrew from them in a sudden hush.
The strong-arm tactics of the oak? The honey-
    Dipped diplomacies of the lilac bush?

In from the cold, her reddened ears were burning
    With what the firelight had been saying of her.
This final urn is wordless now, concerning
    Her ashes and the ashes of her lover.

Under their phrases meaninglessness churn'd;
    Imprisoned in their whispers lay a yell.
Down here we contemplate the deftly-turned
    Newel-posts of the stairway up to hell.

High on the rocks some Ponderosa pine
    Must overlook the jagged valley's floor.
What then must one have witnessed to divine
    That death was just a side-effect of war?

He'd long since put his feet into that part
    Of life from which they could not be withdrawn.
Late blossoms danced, then shook and took to heart
    Summer's long shadows falling on the lawn.

Words of pure winter, yet not pinched nor mean:
    Blue truth can handle a good deal of gray.
Dulled, but incontrovertibly still green,
    The noble laurel holds the cold at bay.

END OF A CHAPTER

…But when true beauty does finally come crashing at us
through the stretched paper of the picturesque, we can
wonder how we had for so long been able to remain dis-
tracted from its absence.

John Hollander

OF CHALLENGE AND OF LOVE

1. HIGH ON OUR TOWER

John Hollander

Elliott Carter
1994

ISMN 979-0-051-93411-9

tow - er _____   Where _____   the   winds _

_____   were _____   Did _____   my _ head _____

_____   turn - ing _____   Turn -

wide _____ stares _____ pinned _____

To a _____ spin -ning world, We burned; _____ my head, Turn -ing to yours On that white _

_____ tow -er, _ Whirled _ high in fire. _____

2. UNDER THE DOME

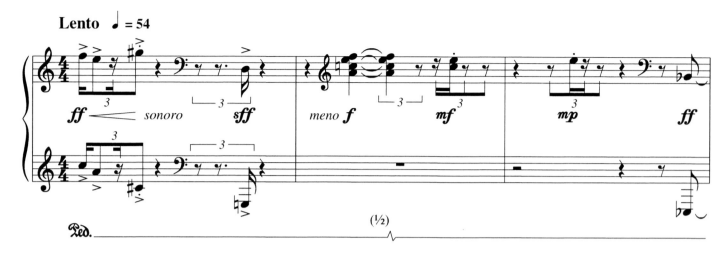

That great, domed cham - ber,

cel - e - brat-ed for its full _____ choir Of ___ ech - oes: _____

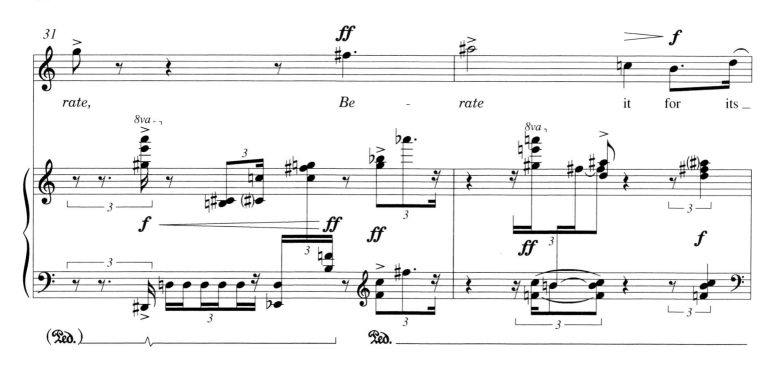

rate,   Be - rate   it   for   its _

_ faults, _   its fran - gi - ble _____ syl - la - bles.

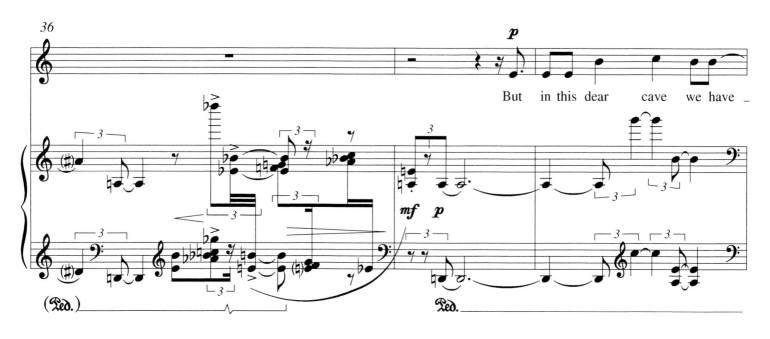

But   in this dear   cave   we have _

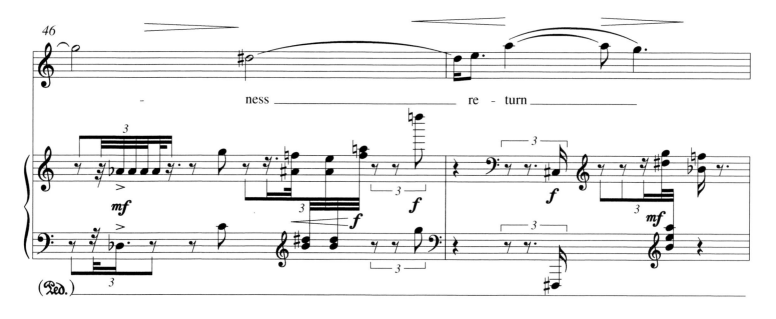

ness _____ re - turn _____

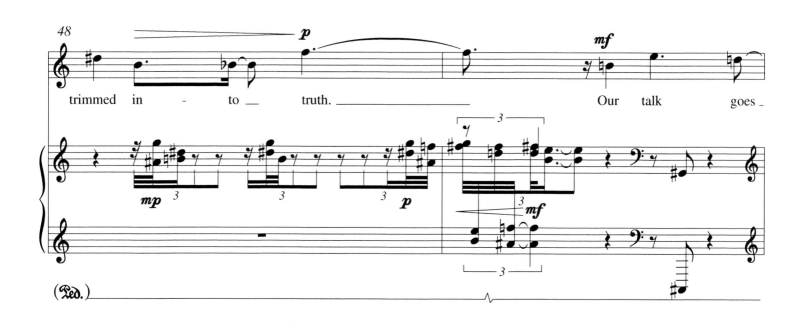

trimmed in - to __ truth. _____ Our talk goes _

_____ un - taunt - ed: ___ these _ are the haunts _____ of __ our

hearts, _____ where I _____ cry

out your name. _____

Hear - ing _____ and ov - er - hear -

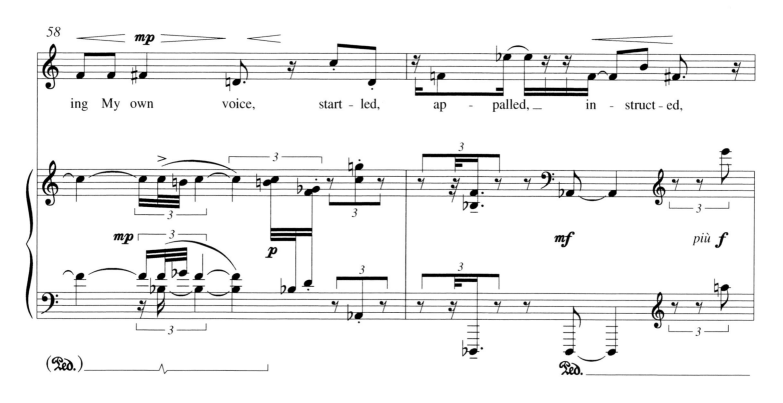

ing My own voice, start - led, ap - palled, _ in - struct - ed,

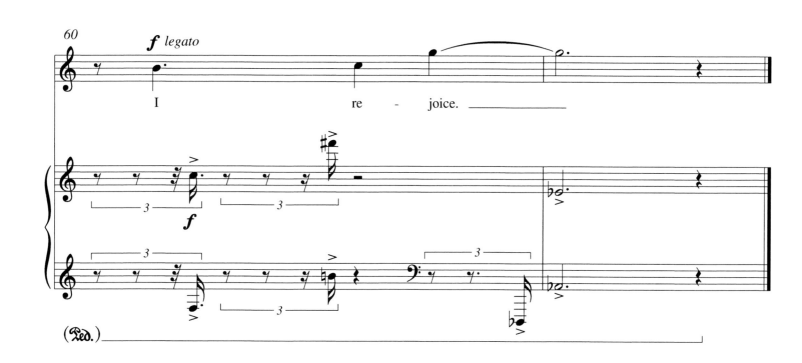

I re - joice. _

3. *AM KLAVIER (at the Piano)*

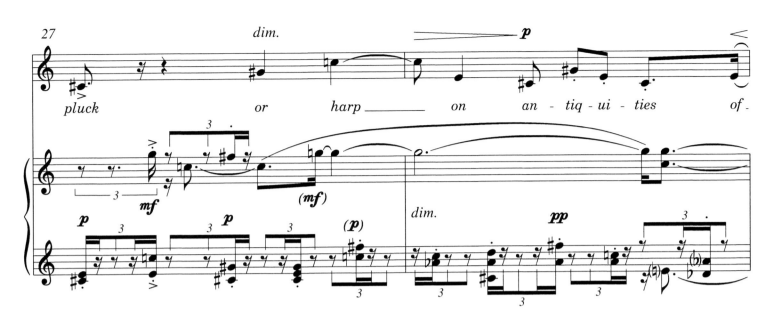

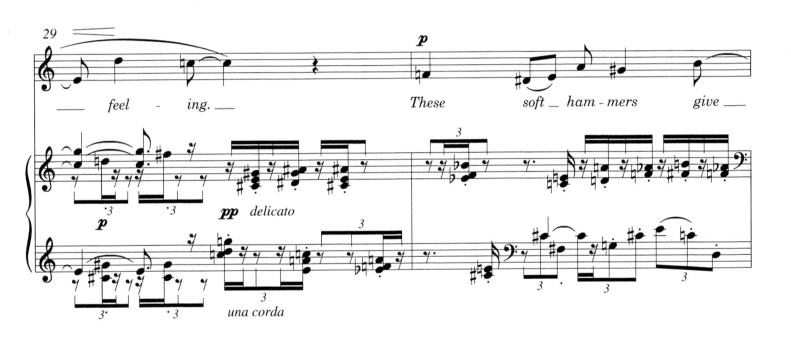

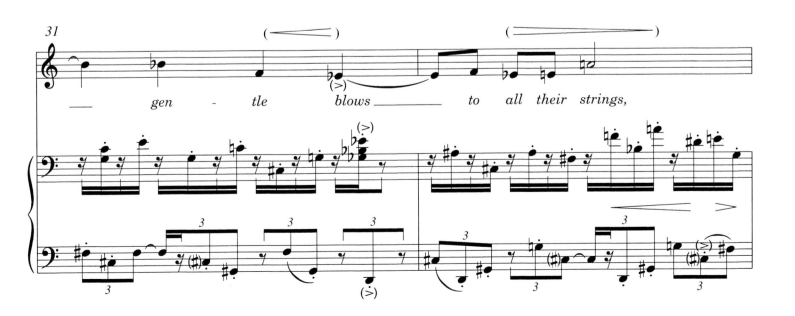

24

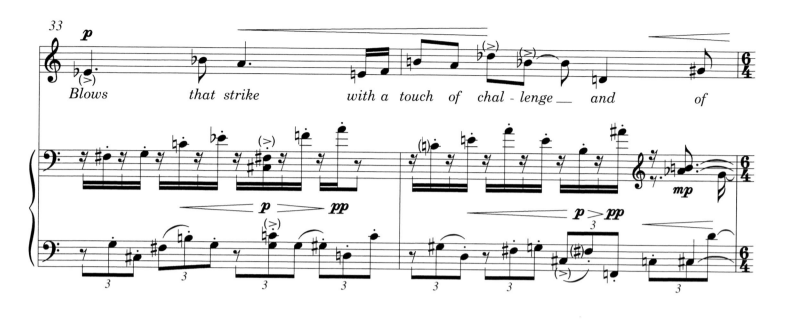

Blows that strike with a touch of chal - lenge ___ and of

love. ___ Thus ___

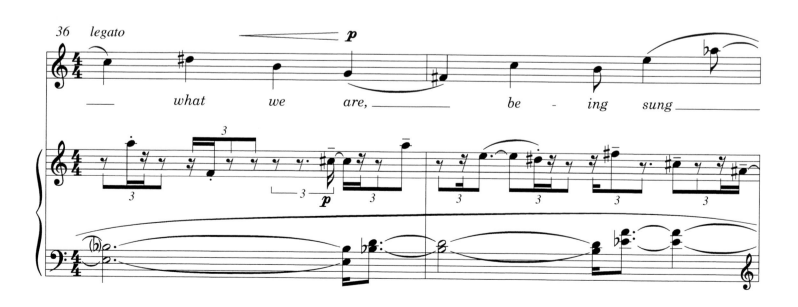

___ what we are, ___ be - ing sung ___

a - gainst _____ what _____ we come _____ To be a

part of, _____ ris - es _____ like _____

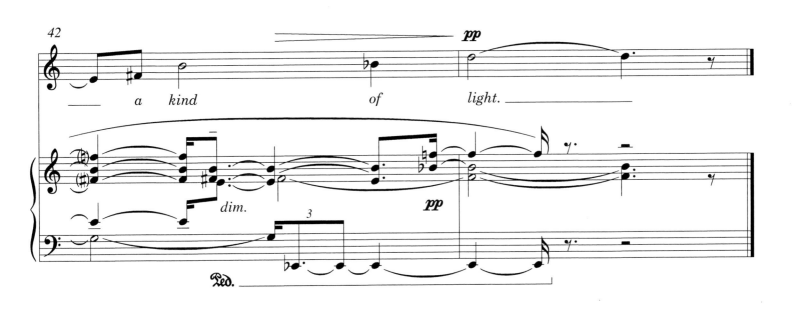

a kind of light. _____

4. QUATRAINS FROM HARP LAKE

had _____ been say - ing of _____

___ her. _____

Mesto

This ___ fi - nal ___ urn _____

36

is word - less now, con - cern - ing

Her ash - es and the ash - es of her

Più mosso

lov - er.

Down here _____ we con - tem - plate the deft - ly - turn'd New -

el - posts of the stair - way up to hell. _____

High _____ on the

40

5. END OF A CHAPTER

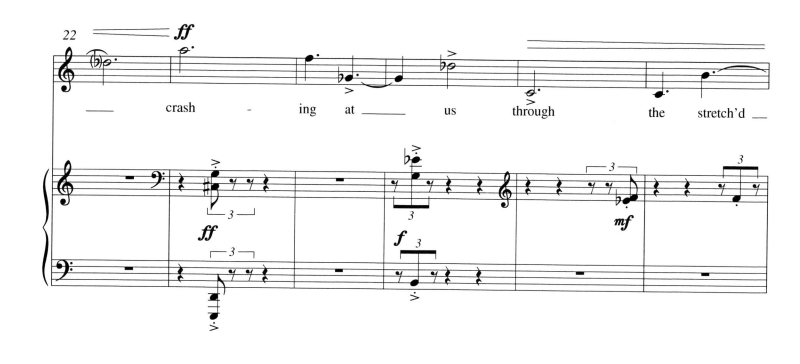

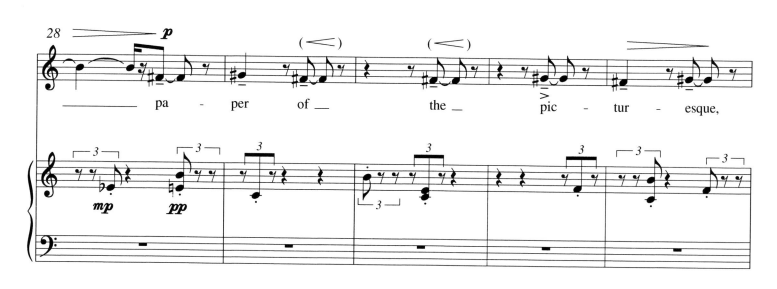

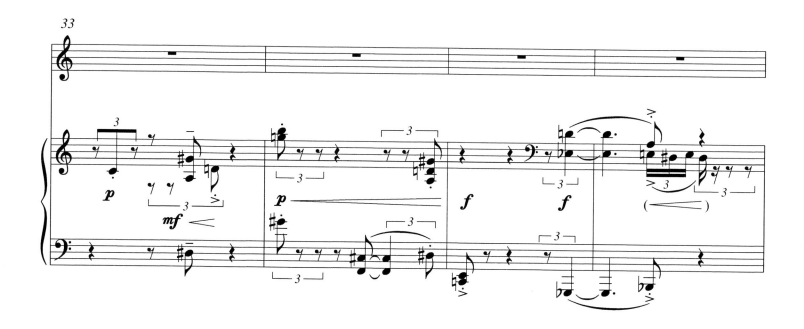

December 31, 1994 NYC